Qu'est-ce que l'histoire,
sinon une fable sur laquelle tout le monde est d'accord?

NAPOLÉON BONAPARTE

The Arkansas Post of Louisiana

Morris S. Arnold

with photographs by Gail K. Arnold

THE UNIVERSITY OF ARKANSAS PRESS
Fayetteville
2017

Manufactured in the Korea
ISBN: 978-1-68226-034-0
e-ISBN: 978-1-61075-616-7

21 20 19 18 5 4 3 2

♾ The paper used in this publication meets the minimum requirements of the American National Standard for Permanence of Paper for Printed Library Materials Z39.48-1984.

Library of Congress Control Number: 2016954396

Design by Ink, Inc., New York.

Eighteenth-century engravings of Quapaw robes: Bibliothèque nationale de France, Estampes Of 4 Petit folio.

The Robe of the Three Villages © musée du quai Branly, Dist. RMN-Grand Palais / Art Resource, NY.

The Robe of the Buffalo Dancers © musée du quai Branly, Dist. RMN-Grand Palais / Art Resource, NY.

Quapaw Treaty: Judicial Records of the Spanish Superior Council, Courtesy of the Louisiana State Museum and the Louisiana Historical Society.

Oath of allegiance to the king of Spain: Judicial Records of the Spanish Superior Council, Courtesy of the Louisiana State Museum and the Louisiana Historical Society.

Captain Balthazar de Villiers's map: Ministerio de Educación, Cultura y Deporte. Archivo General de Indias. AGI, MP-Florida_ Luisiana, 82-Etablissement du poste des Akansas aux Ecores Rouges (1779).

Portraits of Captain Joseph Bernard Vallière d'Hauterive, Charles Melchior de Vilemont, and Marie Félicité Geneviève Vallière are from the Permanent Collection of the Historic Arkansas Museum, Little Rock, Arkansas.

Drawing by Alexandre de Batz, 1735. Gift of the Estate of Belle J. Bushnell. Courtesy of the Peabody Museum of Archaeology and Ethnology, Harvard University, PM# 41-72-10/20 (digital file #60741527).

Portrait of Francis Vigo is used with permission of the Byron R. Lewis Historical Library, Vincennes University.

Pierre Petit de Coulange's commission: The Historic New Orleans Collection, MSS 171 Folder 3.

Portrait of Marie Madeleine Broutin Delinó de Chalmette is courtesy of the Historic New Orleans Collection, acquisition made possible by the Diana Helis Henry Art Fund of the Helis Foundation and the Laussat Society of the Historic New Orleans Collection, acc. no. 2009.0231.1.

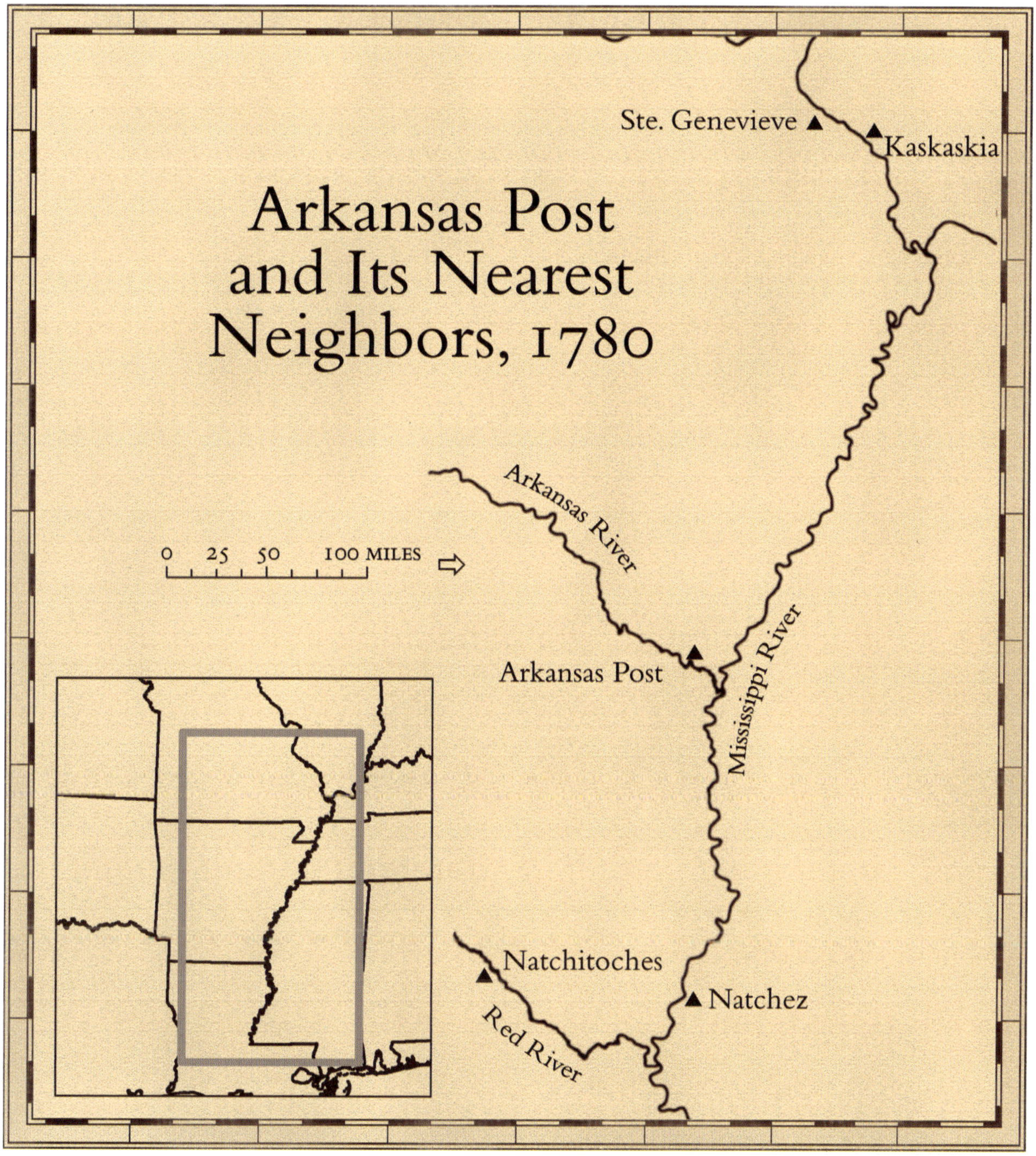

MAP BY JOSEPH SWAIN

Henri de Tonty, 1649–1704. Attributed to Nicolaes Maes.
History Museum of Mobile.

THE ARKANSAS POST OF LOUISIANA was born of René Cavelier de La Salle's grandiose commercial scheme to establish a French crescent of influence in the heart of North America, running from Quebec and Montreal, through the Illinois country, down the Mississippi, and around the Gulf Coast—confining the English colonies to the Eastern seaboard and preventing Spanish intrusions from the south and west. Because La Salle knew that the success of his venture depended on a strong connection with the Quapaw Indians—the French called them the Arkansas—who lived in the very heart of his project near the mouth of the Arkansas River, the first order of business on his imperialist agenda for that region was a trade and military alliance with the tribe. He moved to accomplish this in 1682 when, accoutered with such Gallic pomp and circumstance as he and his small company could muster at the time, he rather fancifully took possession of the whole of Louisiana at one of the Quapaw villages. A more serious effort to effect the alliance occurred in 1686, when Henri de Tonty, La Salle's associate, left six of his men to settle near the Quapaws. This was the first *Poste aux Arkansas* and the first white settlement in what would become Jefferson's Louisiana.

Even among Europe's most remote outposts of empire, the Arkansas Post was an exotic standout. For one thing, though not a few such establishments petered out (the Post did about 1941), not many petered in. The tiny settlement would move about uneasily

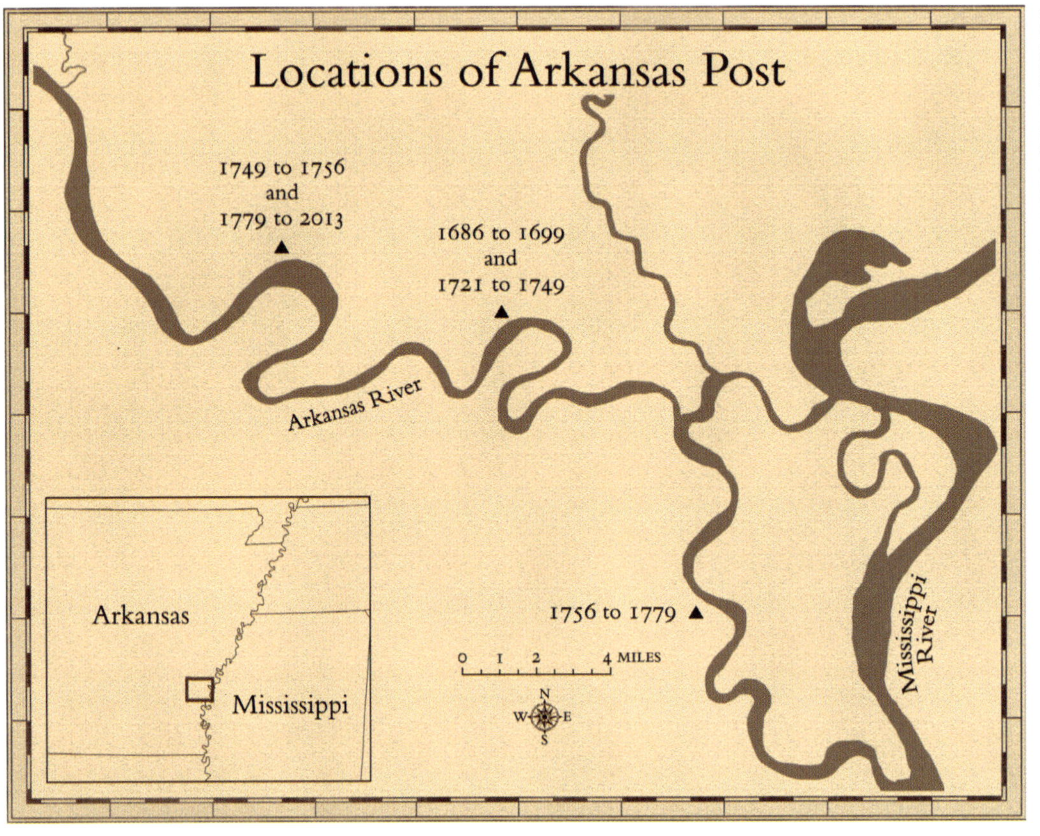

MAP BY JOSEPH SWAIN

and flicker in and out of existence for the better part of a century before finally coming to rest. Tonty's outpost was abandoned by 1699 and was not resurrected until 1721, when it became central to John Law's fantasy of a mid-American empire, a fantasy that had captured the attention of Louis XV's government and a whole horde of investors. But this new Post, located at Tonty's old site, was inconsequential and vulnerable: The Louisiana governor lamented in 1739 that there were only three *habitants* (farmers) there, "who do nothing"; and only ten years later, in 1749, the Chickasaws, in thrall to the westering British expansionists across the Mississippi River, attacked the Post, killed six male settlers, and carried off a number of women and children. The troops and the settlement immediately moved upriver a few miles, closer to the Quapaw villages, for better security, to the high ground that

Reconstructed Fort St. Jean Baptiste, Natchitoches. Photo by Gail K. Arnold.

the French called *Écores Rouges* (Red Bluffs). There, the Louisiana government raised the most elaborate fort ever built in the Arkansas country and reinforced the garrison. (The new fort must have borne a strong resemblance to Fort St. Jean Baptiste, which was built in Natchitoches in 1732 and has been reconstructed.) But this seemingly secure reincarnation of the Post proved to be very short-lived. In 1756, barely four years after the new fort was finished, the Post, because of the Seven Years' War, had to relocate yet again. It moved downriver into what is now Desha County, well past its old location and near the Mississippi, to be more convenient to the military convoys plying the great waterway. At the time, though it sheltered only about fifty people, free and slave, there was no other European settlement between Natchez and Ste. Genevieve, a stretch of more than 800 miles along the river, so the Post was important precisely because it was out in the middle of nowhere.

The Post's extreme instability of course discouraged settlers with more permanent ambitions and during its first one hundred years its population turned over completely every twenty years—perhaps even more frequently than that. The Post's Desha County site, moreover, while admittedly more convenient to travelers on the colony's main artery, provided no inducement to settlement because it was uncongenial to *habitants*. It was directly in the Mississippi floodplain, and almost every year the waters of the mighty river overwhelmed such houses as there were at the Post, though they were built on six-foot stilts; even the fort, on the highest ground available, sometimes stood and swam in two feet of water. Needless to say, producing a reliable crop there, even with a hastily thrown-up levee, was impossible, so the few residents of the Post were almost all merchants. Their main business was supplying itinerant hunters on credit, taking their products as payment, and trading those products to large merchant houses in New Orleans for goods, beginning the credit cycle again. The state of the agricultural and mechanical arts was so backward that when Alexandre Chevalier DeClouet took command of the Post in 1768, the *habitants* did not even have the outdoor ovens for baking bread that had been a common feature of every other town in the colony for decades. He did finally succeed in getting four of these built, but he could not coax the *habitants* into organizing a common grain field and Post residents found themselves in such dire straits that they were reduced to trading liquor to the Quapaws for maize.

The Quapaws were a Deghia Siouxan people. Their origin narrative recounts that in the sixteenth century their enemies had driven them into the Arkansas country from their ancestral

Alexandre Chevalier DeClouet, 1727–1789, ca. 1775. Dupré Library of the University of Louisiana at Lafayette.

Outdoor oven, reconstructed Fort St. Jean Baptiste, Natchitoches.
Photo by Gail K. Arnold.

lands along the Ohio River. They and their Deghia cousins, the Osages, Omahas, Poncas, and Kansas, speak closely related languages and all these tribes share similar accounts of a migration, but the question of when the Quapaws arrived in Arkansas is a matter of considerable controversy. What is important for present purposes is that they were in place when La Salle ventured down the Mississippi River. They received him and his company with more than a little enthusiasm, partly because they were looking for markets in general, but principally because they wanted guns to defend themselves against the Chickasaws who were affected to the English to the east of the great river.

La Salle's plan to confine the English to the eastern part of the continent fit completely with Quapaw ambitions. A common foe often provides a unifying force in human affairs: The enemy of my enemy is my friend. La Salle offered the Quapaws all kinds of assurances about how advantageous an alliance with the French would be and promised that many Frenchmen would soon come to settle among them to defend them from the Chickasaws, blandishments that proved hollow in the event. The Quapaws' need of the French, however, deepened as time went on, since a combination of English-inspired slave-raiding by the Chickasaws and devastating losses from smallpox and other diseases reduced their population from perhaps ten thousand in 1680 to around one thousand in 1720.

Official French and Spanish accounts of the Quapaws were written for military, political, or commercial purposes, and so they tended to emphasize the Quapaws' prowess as hunters and warriors and their attachment to the European influence—and, indeed, the relations between the two peoples were mostly cordial and harmonious during the 120 years or so that they shared the Arkansas region. What does not come through in those accounts, though, are some of the more pacific attributes of the tribe. The Quapaws were accomplished horticulturists, and produced corn, beans, squash, and melons in quantities that the French in the environs soon learned to be glad of. The Quapaws were also very creative artists and their painted buffalo, elk, and deer skins were in much demand among the Indian nations because of their engaging designs and striking beauty. Indian men wore them as robes and they served as dividers in long houses, even as tablecloths.

A number of large examples of these remarkable eighteenth-century hide paintings, upwards of six or seven, survive in French museums, probably traded or given to Post residents or wayfarers passing through the Quapaw country. They are all extraordinarily colorful and painterly.

Eighteenth-century engravings of Quapaw robes, ca. 1750. Bibliothèque nationale de France, Paris.

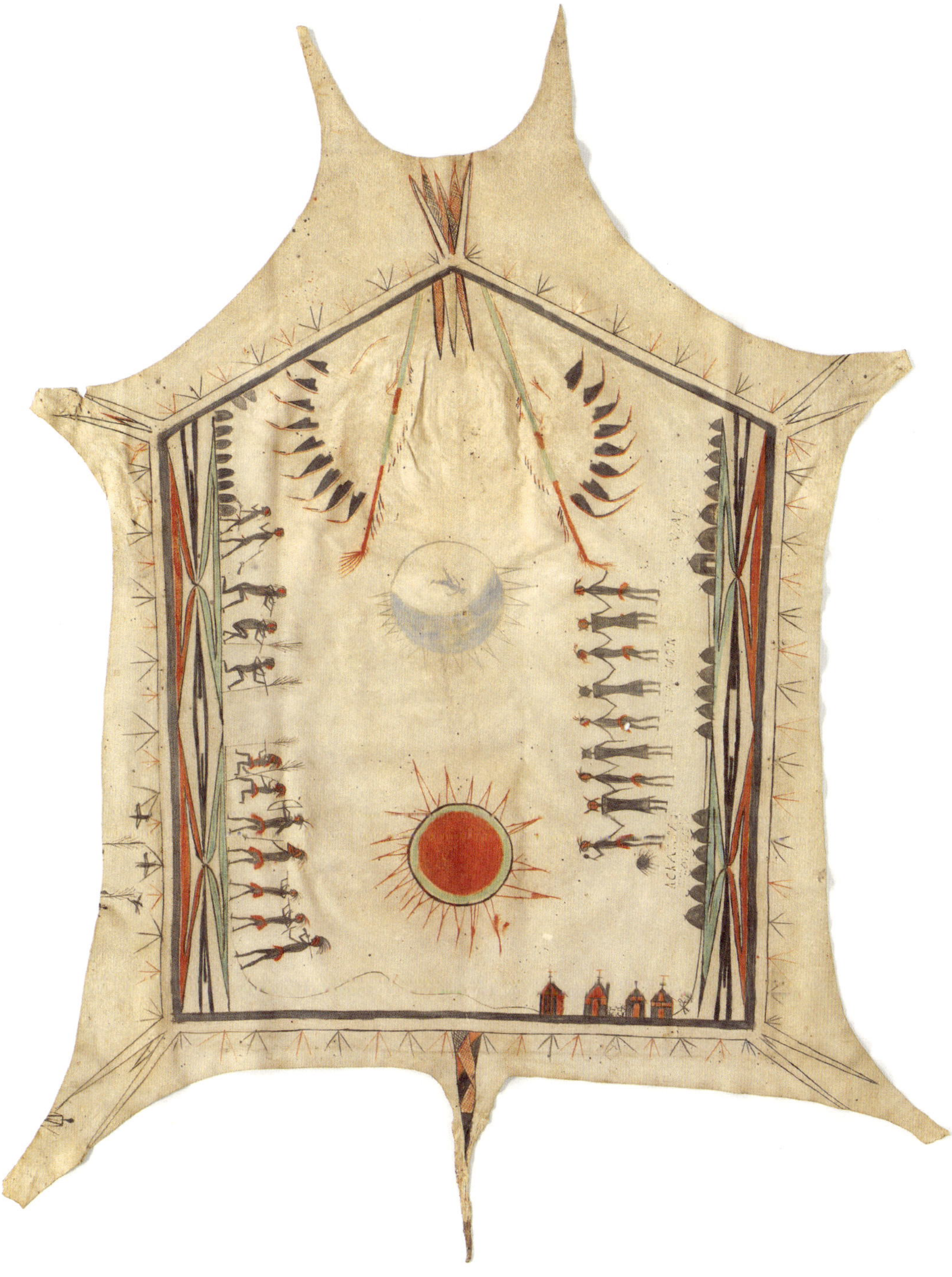

The Robe of the Three Villages, ca. 1740–50.
Musée du quai Branly—Jacques Chirac, Paris.

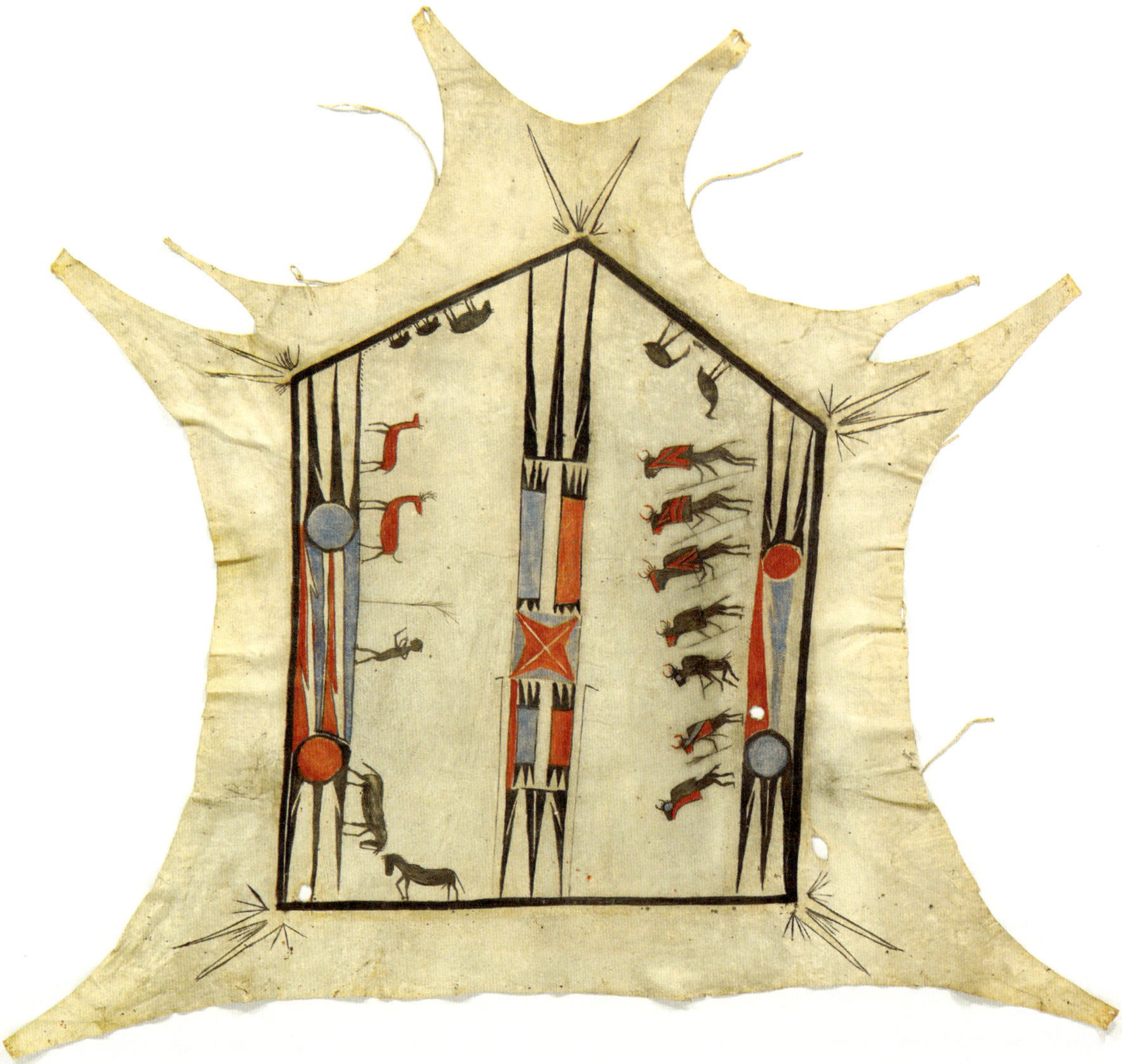

Robe of the Buffalo Dancers, ca. 1750.
Musée du quai Branly—Jacques Chirac, Paris.

Detail from the Robe of the Three Villages, depicting Arkansas Post and a Quapaw village.

Detail from the Robe of the Buffalo Dancers.

The most vivid Quapaw painting extant depicts Quapaw men and women dancing in their villages to celebrate a victory over the Chickasaws around 1740 or 1750. Most remarkable of all, perhaps, it features the buildings of Arkansas Post itself, the only rendition of the colonial settlement that we have. It shows the jail, the powder house, the soldiers' barracks, and the commandant's house—this last quite possibly the house where one Marie Françoise Petit de Coulange was born and where Marie Madeleine Broutin Delinó de Chalmette would later live. (More on them later.) Another of these robes features members of the tribe dressed up as buffalos for the hunt, and contains very appealing figures of bears, deer, cranes, and horses.

The French, and then the Spanish in their turn, strove mightily to keep the Quapaws close because of their strategic location in the heart of the Mississippi valley and because, before long, they became the only tribe living in the region. To maintain this important alliance, the Louisiana government undertook to provide the Quapaws with an annual gift of guns, ammunition, and other supplies, gave medals to chiefs to reward meritorious service, and furnished the tribe with an interpreter—an Indian agent, essentially—and with a gunsmith to keep their weapons in good order.

The Quapaws took all this in stride and remained attached, or at least not inimical, to their European neighbors; but they never regarded themselves as subjects and the Louisiana government did not even pretend that they were. Colonial officials, for instance, never made any serious efforts to apply European law to the Quapaws and respected their sovereignty in other ways. For reasons of economy, moreover, the French made only episodic and largely

Spanish medal awarded to Quapaw chief, bearing the likeness of King Carlos III of Spain, ca. 1775. Private collection of Supernaw family.

ineffective efforts to convert the Indians to Christianity, and the Spanish, to preserve commercial harmony, deliberately eschewed the old mission-and-fort brand of imperialism that they were even then pursuing in California. This hands-off attitude must have greatly enhanced the Quapaws' sense of identity and independence.

In truth, the church had very little influence in colonial Arkansas even on the Europeans there because of the nature and small size of the Post population. Although there was a priest resident at the Arkansas as early as 1700, he was soon martyred, and for most of the eighteenth century the French of the Arkansas region had to be content with episodic visits from peripatetic missionaries. To this general picture of neglect there were two main exceptions. About 1752, first of all, the Jesuit Father Louis Carette came to the Post as resident missionary and was given a position of prominence, for a large building constructed there in about the same year contained a chapel and living quarters for the priest and for the commandant. This arrangement could only have created an impression of a certain equality between church and state, though the priest lived in only one room while the commandant had two. When the post moved downriver in 1756, however, no chapel was provided, and the priest was segregated in a separate one-room building that doubled as his chamber and chapel. This annoyed Father Carette greatly, but he persevered there for two more years until an event that he considered seriously sacrilegious finally precipitated his departure.

It would be almost forty years before the Post saw another regular curé. In 1796, Father Pierre Janin, who had made the mistake of telling his bishop that he did not like big cities, found himself assigned to the remote post of Los Arcos, as the Spanish called Arkansas Post, with the job of establishing the first canonical parish ever erected there. He called it the parish of St. Stephen, because St. Stephen was the name of the fort built at the Post in 1792; the commandant had given the fort that name to flatter the governor, Esteban (i.e., Stephen) Miró. Father Janin brought along some vestments with him and, from the bishop's own chapel in New Orleans, an altar, two brass candle sticks, a china baptismal font, some glass cruets, and three purificators. Unfortunately for the small cadre of the devout at the Post, their priest was called away in 1799 to the more populous and prestigious parish in St. Louis, and the Louisiana church was never able to find a replacement to tend the Arkansas flock.

After the Louisiana regime changed from French to Spanish in 1768, the Quapaws signed on to a kind of treaty with the new government that highlighted their independence, for it obligated them only to "listen to" what the Louisiana governor and Arkansas commandant had to say; thus they undertook to do more

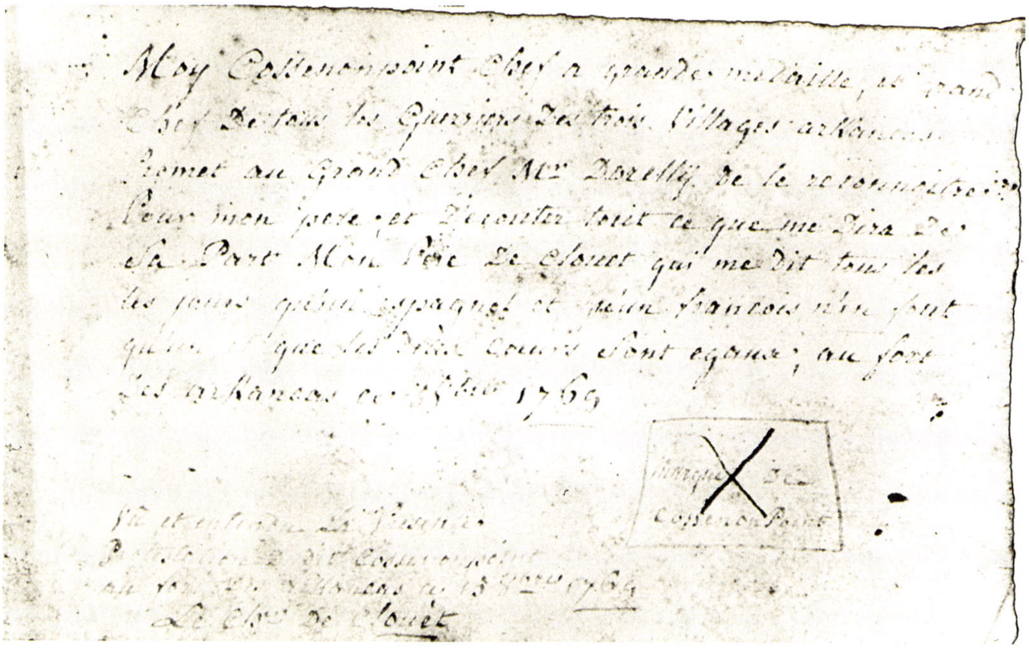

Quapaw Treaty, 15 October 1769. Louisiana State Museum, New Orleans.

than merely hear but less than blindly heed. In stark contrast, the French *habitants* living at the Post when it changed hands took an oath of allegiance that pledged their lives and all their worldly goods to His Most Catholic Majesty (that is, the king of Spain) and dedicated themselves to his supreme royal will.

Though the Quapaws and their European neighbors maintained separate sovereignties, their interdependence manifested itself in a number of ways, most obviously in the fact that their towns remained close to each other. The Quapaws had even moved downriver with the French in 1756, and in the 1770s the residents of the Post and the Quapaws collaborated in building a road to join the Spanish settlement with the Indian villages for purposes of defense and trade. There was also a certain amount of intermarriage between the French and the Quapaws, but its extent remains more than a little obscure.

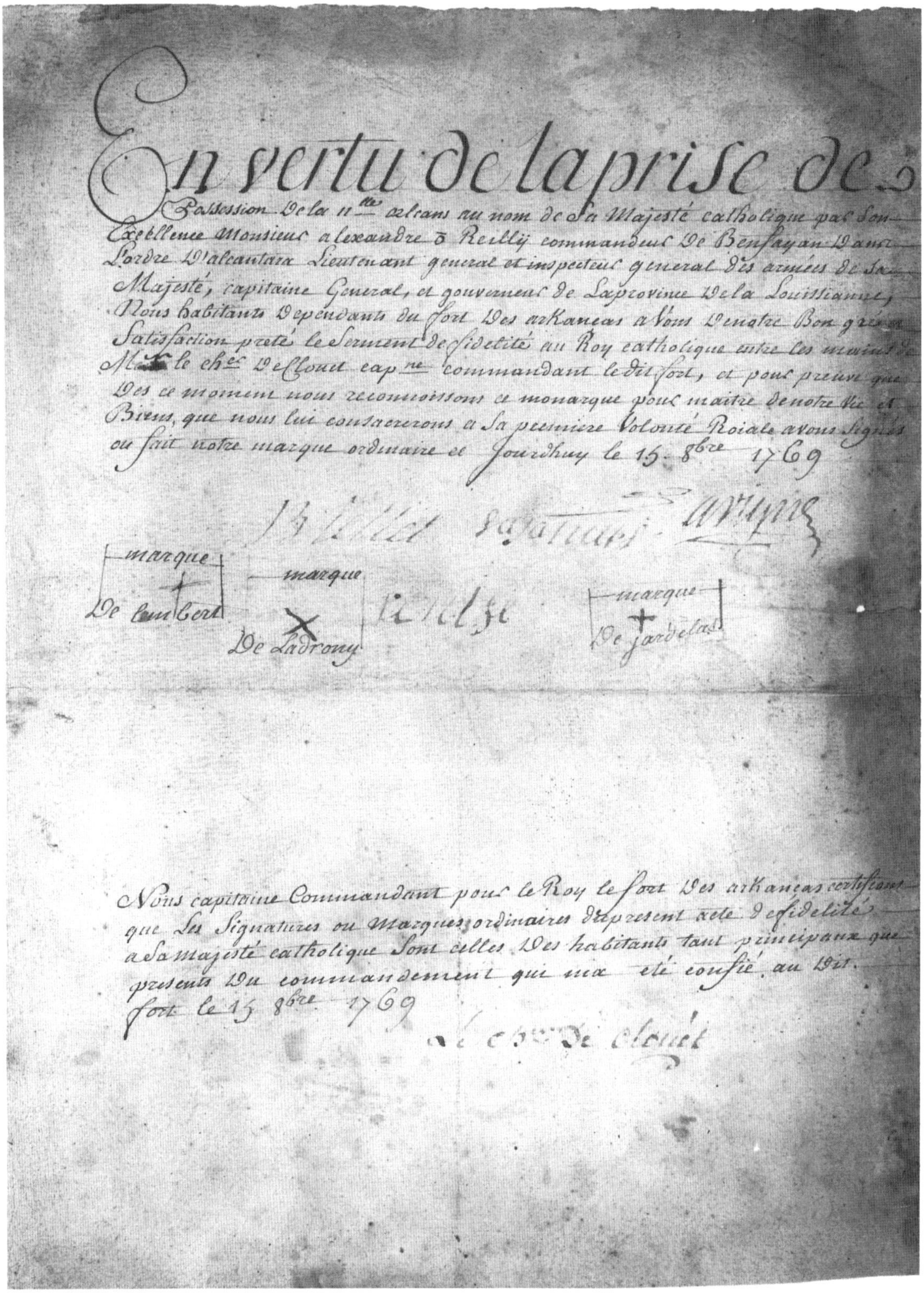

En vertu de la prise de possession de la 11e dernier au nom de Sa Majesté catholique par Son Excellence Monsieur Alexandre O Reilly commandeur de Benfayan dans l'ordre d'Alcantara Lieutenant general et inspecteur general des armées de Sa Majesté, capitaine General, et gouverneur de la province de la Louissianne, Nous habitants dependants du fort des Arkancas avons de notre bon gré et satisfaction preté le serment de fidelité au Roy catholique entre les mains de Mr le chev. de Clouet capne commandant le dit fort, et pour preuve que des ce moment nous reconnoissons ce monarque pour maitre de notre vie et biens, que nous lui consacrerons a sa premiere volonté Roiale avons signés ou fait notre marque ordinaire ce jourdhuy le 15 8bre 1769

marque + De Lambert

marque X De Ladrony

marque + De Jardelas

Nous capitaine Commandant pour le Roy le fort des Arkancas certifions que les signatures ou marques ordinaires du present acte de fidelité a Sa Majesté catholique sont celles des habitants tant principaux que presents du commandement qui m'a eté confié au dit fort le 15 8bre 1769

Le chev. de Clouet

Oath of allegiance to the king of Spain taken by the *habitants* of Arkansas Post, 15 October 1769. Louisiana State Museum, New Orleans.

Detail of a map of the Mississippi River, showing the proximity of Arkansas Post (Arkansas) and a Quapaw village (Village Indien), 1796. Bibliothèque nationale, Paris.

In 1779, a particularly devastating flood submerged the Post, destroying all the crops, drowning most of the livestock, and rendering the better part of the houses there forever uninhabitable. Parts of the fort's curtain wall had collapsed and the well had caved in. A large number of the Post's residents had resolved to abandon the place altogether and move down to New Orleans. So Captain Balthazar de Villiers, with the Quapaws fully agreed that it was past time to leave, ordered the denizens of his hapless little slough of despond to pull up stakes yet again and return to *Écores Rouges* to try to begin anew. Villiers had despised his duty station for some time, and for obvious reasons, and he was not the least bit reticent about saying so. He once called the Post *le réduit le plus désagréable de l'univers*—the most disagreeable hole in the universe. There were only fifty white people and eleven black slaves

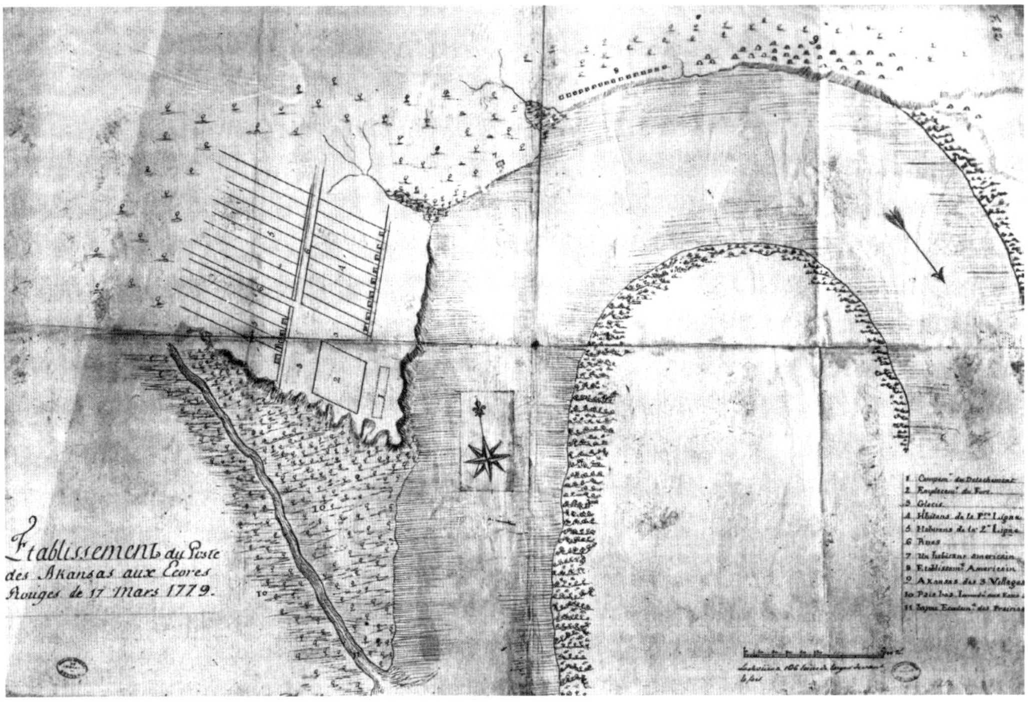

Captain Balthazar de Villiers's map of Arkansas Post, 1779.
Archivo General de Las Indias, Seville.

residing at the Post when Villiers decided to forsake the aqueous ruin for higher ground, and many contemporaries agreed with his assessment of the place. In 1766, an English traveler on the Mississippi, on passing the mouth of the Arkansas River, had sniffed that "the few Banditti at the Arkansas did not deserve the name of settlement." To his new situation, Villiers predicted, he could attract respectable agrarian settlers who would fashion a more permanent attachment to the place and elevate its reputation.

Time would reveal that the Post had finally found a permanent situation, and Villiers's 1779 map of his new circumstances, together with the animated report that he sent the governor describing the settlement's prospects, gave promise of a prosperous future. In fact, there was every reason to be extremely optimistic. Within a year of the Post's relocation, nine American families had arrived from Illinois and a large number of families from South Carolina had petitioned for permission to settle. Villiers must have thought himself on the verge of a considerable success, but events associated with the American Revolution soon overtook him. The French and the Spanish had aligned themselves against the English in the conflict, not because they favored the American anti-monarchist cause in the abstract, but because their imperialist ambitions ran counter to those of the British. So the Spanish moved against and captured the English settlements at Baton Rouge, Natchez, Mobile, and Pensacola, and laid claim to and annexed West Florida.

In 1782, two Hessian deserters (members of the Post garrison) and several refugees from the American Revolution who lived at the Post plotted to open the gates of the fort to allow British sympathizers to enter and butcher the troops. By the end of the year, there were only ten *habitants* and their families remaining at the Post. Many settlers no doubt had abandoned the place because they feared a British attack; others had probably felt unwelcome, or had been asked to leave, because they were suspected of harboring treasonous thoughts. Villiers, his ambitions unrealized, died penniless soon after, ruined by a horde of faithless debtors, including recently arrived American refugees who had taken his goods on credit and disappeared into the woods. In his will, Villiers remembered to leave his son a silver-plated musket, a memento of palmier days.

The full force of the American Revolution, perhaps like many other things, came late to Arkansas Post, but when it arrived, it arrived with a bang. The English and their Chickasaw allies had not sat idly by while the Spanish military actions in West Florida

Cannon at reconstructed Fort Carlos III, Arkansas Post National Memorial. Photo by Gail K. Arnold.

raged against them, and they regularly harassed and raided the Spanish merchant and military craft that plied the Mississippi. One of these British pirates, a partisan named James Colbert, a rich merchant and planter who lived among and married into the Chickasaw tribe, had been threatening to attack the Post itself. On 17 April 1783, though preliminary treaties had already called for hostilities to cease, he proved he was by no means all bluster. His force of perhaps seventy men—mostly Englishmen and *métis* (English-Chickasaw mixed bloods), along with a few black slaves—rowed up the Arkansas River, slipped past the Quapaw villages, and in the early morning struck the Post.

The complete surprise that Colbert was able to carry off earned him some early successes. His men killed two Spanish sentinels and captured six soldiers, six of the town's ten *habitant* families, and some slaves. The raiders then laid siege to the fort, where the garrison had only recently been reinforced to about seventy soldiers. During the battle, which lasted a number of hours, fusillades from Colbert's carbines raked the fort, which answered with muskets and as many as three hundred cannon rounds from its palisades and ramparts. The insurgents, trying to bluff the defenders into surrendering, claimed that they had a cannon on the way themselves, but, in fact, as soon became plain, they did not. After a kind of draw had ensued, a squadron of Spanish soldiers, along with four Quapaw warriors who had just coincidentally been trapped inside when the battle was joined, suddenly sallied forth from their redoubt with such a noisy violence that the enemy thought the entire Quapaw nation had been set upon them.

Panicked, the intruders beat an unruly retreat, pursued eventually by Captain Joseph Vallière, who happened to be near the Post at the right moment, at the head of a group of Spanish soldiers and Quapaws. He caught up with Colbert's forces, routed them, and rescued some of the captives. Colbert himself had long since escaped to tout his version of events, no doubt somewhat different from the facts, but a few months later he died from a fall from his horse—an indecorous but not altogether dishonorable demise. Captain Vallière went on to serve as the Post's commandant from 1787 to 1790. His portrait shows him decked out in a bicorne colonial captain's hat festooned with the white-and-red alliance cockade—the white for France, the red for Spain—that French and Spanish officers wore during their service in the American Revolution.

Though individual Quapaws had played an important part in saving the day for the Spanish, and members of the tribe had participated in the operations following the attack, the Quapaw tribe itself had remained officially aloof while the battle was waged.

Joseph Vallière, 1742–1797, ca 1783.
Historic Arkansas Museum, Little Rock.

When the Arkansas commandant angrily upbraided Great Chief Angaska for his neglect, and even accused the tribe of conniving in the attack, the chief sought to excuse himself by claiming that Colbert had deceived him and concealed his true intentions. Another chief was much blunter: He said that it was a white man's war and the Quapaws had not been exactly anxious to take sides. It is not likely that the Quapaws had any great affection for the American colonists anyway, given their demonstrated expansionist tendencies, of which the Quapaws were well aware. The Quapaws' aloofness during Colbert's raid provides an excellent example of how the tribe habitually followed an independent foreign policy. Besides, as Europeans frequently noted, the Quapaw polity, unlike theirs, did not have any one person who could determine its course and command instant obedience. Rallying the tribal community to war was a matter for study and consensus, not something that can readily occur in response to sudden events.

A French-Quapaw *métis* named Saracen, however, helped ease the rift between the tribe and the Spanish, and earned himself a large measure of gratitude from the Post population—indeed, he achieved the status of a hero. He was one of the Quapaws who had caused Colbert's forces to turn tail and run. More than that, he had set upon some of the invaders, thrown a spear into their midst, and rescued the children of a Spanish officer whose family had been captured in the raid. St. Joseph's Church in Pine Bluff once had a window that commemorated Saracen and his derring-do, and some local citizens had even proposed that a statue of him be erected in town in gratitude for his friendship to the whites.

In time, and in its more hospitable location, civil society at the Post did finally improve somewhat. One of the first wheat crops was produced at the Post in 1787 when three French families from the Illinois country, fleeing American rule, particularly the Northwest Ordinance which abolished slavery, migrated to Arkansas along with their horse-powered grist mills. These were the first mills of record at the Post. By 1791, not even a decade after Villiers had relinquished his command, the Post's population had risen to 114 white people, 37 black and mulatto slaves, and eight *métis* of French and Indian descent. Of the 27 households, 16 were headed by farmers (*cultivateurs*). But three of the farm families owned over half the slaves, and the largest slave owner was the widow Ménard who was a merchant and produced no crop at all. The gross agricultural product of the town was quite small, only about 300 *minots* of wheat and 4,600 *minots* of corn. (A *minot* was a little more than a bushel.) This output nevertheless represented a considerable improvement over what the *habitants* had been able to produce in the lowlands a few years earlier. Five merchant families still lived at the Post, though the dozen or so farmers who produced a crop did outnumber them. A carpenter and a *menuisier* (joiner or cabinetmaker) were also resident, evidence of progress in the material environment. The *menuisier* probably fashioned barrels for exporting agricultural goods, performed finishing work on buildings, and made furniture. Though there was no tailor, itinerant tailors paid occasional visits to the Post and two resident *métis* women offered their services as seamstresses.

Seven years later, in 1798, the last available census for the colonial period records a population just shy of 400 at the Post—more than double that in 1791—including three free people of color and 56 mulatto and black slaves. The census unfortunately does not give residents' occupations. There were now 30 families reporting a crop, but almost half grew only corn, and the corn crop was only half what it had been in 1791. This was probably barely sufficient to sustain the Post's people and animals. Four farmers produced the bulk of the Post's 947 *minots* of wheat, about half the 1793 wheat crop and probably not enough to supply local needs. Tobacco became a cash crop at the Arkansas in 1793, in response perhaps to hopes that the Spanish would subsidize it. But by 1798, after it had become clear that no governmental inducements were forthcoming, tobacco production had plunged to a mere 200 *carottes* (a *carotte* was a five-pound plug), less than a quarter of the output recorded four years before. The cash value of the crops grown in 1798 was only 60 percent of the value of the crop produced in 1791. So, though the agricultural and mechanical arts had improved somewhat following Villiers's relocation of the settlement, the small and steadily dwindling output of the Post during the waning years of the colonial era shows that his dream of a significant agrarian establishment at the Arkansas had eluded him.

Nevertheless, the 1790s, when Ignace Delinó de Chalmette and Charles de Vilemont commanded at the Post, were certainly the heyday of the colonial town, if it had one. The Spanish government was anxious to increase the population at and around the Post, and in 1795 *Le Moniteur de La Louisiane*, the New Orleans newspaper, crowed that the establishment of the Spanish fort *San Fernando de Las Barrancas* at the current site of Memphis would greatly encourage immigration to the Arkansas district. The next year, Governor Corondelet assured Captain Vilemont that his "settlement was going to become very considerable." Though all this boosterism was more than a little overblown, the Post's population probably tripled during the 1790s. And the evaluations of the settlement that

Charles Melchior de Vilemont, 1762–1822, ca. 1775.
Historic Arkansas Museum, Little Rock.

some visitors offered during that decade were a good deal more positive than previous evaluations had been when the little outpost had languished in its downriver sink. For instance, in 1793 when the Spanish war galiot *La Flecha* (*The Arrow*) put in at the Post, its captain, Pedro Rousseau, reported that the village, which was upriver

Badin-Roque house, Natchitoches, built early nineteenth century. Photo by Gail K. Arnold.

from the fort, contained "about thirty houses with galleries around, roofed with shingles, which formed two streets." These two streets are doubtless the *rues* that Villiers had laid out and marked off on his 1779 map; they are probably also the Front Street and Main Street of the early nineteenth-century American settlement. Downriver, below the fort, Rousseau said, were "a dozen quite pretty houses [on plots] of four-by-four arpents [a linear arpent was 192 feet], where there are very beautiful fields of wheat on the highlands."

In 1796, George-Henri-Victor Collot, a French spy on a reconnaissance mission in the Mississippi valley, had some qualified praise for the state of agriculture at the Post. "A single farm," Collot wrote, "belonging to Mr. Wolf, a German, evinced what might be expected from a country this fertile. He was employed in gathering in his corn harvest, which had yielded him two hundred fold." Collot opined that the "quality of the wheat was

Storekeeper's house, reconstructed Fort St. Jean Baptiste, Natchitoches. Photo by Gail K. Arnold.

certainly equal to that of the best departments of France; which leaves no doubt, that under a government favorable to agriculture, this cultivation would be attended with great success."

Residents and sojourners at the Post during its first three incarnations carped constantly about the primitive housing conditions that they had to endure. In 1758, for instance, Étienne Layssard, who held the exalted title of keeper of the king's storehouse, complained bitterly to the governor of Louisiana of his desperate circumstances. "My wife and I," he wrote, "four children, five slaves, a dog, a cat, and chickens live in a small house 25 feet long and 16 feet wide, with one little fireplace to warm us all." Father Vitry had registered a similar lament in 1739 when describing the accommodation of a fellow religious at the Post's first site. It was, he said, "a makeshift hut," and though he had previously "lived

Bequette-Ribault house, Ste. Genevieve, with the *grand champ* in the background, built ca. 1810. Photo by Gail K. Arnold.

Tauzin-Wells house, Natchitoches, built 1776.
Photo by Gail K. Arnold.

in such houses . . . nowhere did [he] have so much fresh air. The house is full of cracks from top to bottom."

But in its final location, as the mercantile importance of the Post grew and agriculture improved modestly, more substantial houses appeared, particularly, as Captain Rousseau had noted, the distinctive creole colonial Louisiana house that featured surrounding galleries. These houses typically had double-pitch hipped roofs and casement windows. Unlike the horizontal-log houses of the American frontier, colonial Louisiana houses were built of upright posts set either in the ground (*poteaux-en-terre*) or on a wooden sill (*poteaux-sur-solle*) that provided a kind of foundation. The nogging material used to fill in between the posts was usually *bousillage*, a mixture of mud, straw, and perhaps some buffalo hair.

An average colonial house in Natchitoches and Ste. Genevieve, the Post's nearest neighbors for most of the eighteenth century, contained respectively about 450 and 600 square feet, but running galleries could double the available living space, at least in the more temperate months. The average house at the Post was of comparable size, comprising about 550 square feet, but some were a good deal more commodious. For instance, Pierre LeFevre, a leading merchant, had a *colombage* house of almost 800 square feet, with a gallery all around it, about the same size as the Bequette-Ribault house in Ste. Genevieve, but smaller than the Bolduc house in the same town. Though LeFevre's is the largest colonial Arkansas dwelling on record, it is quite likely that there were one or two bigger ones, belonging to prosperous merchants like François Ménard, who was the richest man at the Post in the 1780s. Ménard even owned a house in New Orleans, and his visits there would have acquainted him with the latest architectural fashions.

Bolduc house, Ste. Genevieve, built 1793.
Photo by Gail K. Arnold.

Back view of Bolduc house, showing the kitchen garden.
Photo by Gail K. Arnold.

Church at reconstructed Fort St. Jean Baptiste, Natchitoches.
Photo by Gail K. Arnold.

And in 1809, only five years after the Americans took over the fort at the Post, the merchant James Scull contracted for an impressive house of 1,550 square feet with a ten-foot gallery on all sides. Probably this building was to serve Scull both as a dwelling and a store. The grander of these colonial homesteads were surrounded by stockade fences that also enclosed outbuildings, separate kitch-

Joseph Vallière, 1742–1797, ca. 1790.
Historic Arkansas Museum, Little Rock.

ens, kitchen gardens, orchards, even sawmills and gristmills. The stockades served mainly to fence out the farm animals, which were branded and allowed to range freely in the woods and on the prairies.

It is plain from this that some few of Arkansas's colonial denizens had achieved a reasonably comfortable standard of living in the waning days of Spanish rule. John James Audubon, the famous painter and ornithologist, though he was very critical of conditions at the 1820 Post, allowed that in the time that "the French and Spanish kept it," the Post of Arkansas "could have been called an agreable [sic] small town." This late-blooming version of the Post, though, was no redoubt of French civilization. As we saw, the first canonical parish at the settlement, erected there in 1796, more than a century after Tonty established the first Post, failed in 1799. The parish of St. Stephen was hardly a flourishing affair anyway: The church building was only 180 feet square and the priest lived in a 6-by-8-foot cell attached to it; about a dozen families provided the church's main support. Thereafter,

Marie Félicité Vallière de Vaugine, 1770–1806, ca. 1790.
Attributed to José Salazar. Historic Arkansas Museum, Little Rock.

Ursuline Convent, New Orleans, built 1753.
Photo by Gail K. Arnold.

the faithful of the Arkansas had to be content with occasional visits from wandering missionary priests, as they had had to do for the most part during the entire eighteenth century. What is more, there was no physician or surgeon readily available to Post residents, nor was there a schoolmaster—at least none has left a trace in the record. Books were scarce, though the priests and some of the commandants had small collections of them. Post residents seeking formal educational opportunities for their children would have had to look elsewhere. Don Joseph Vallière's daughter, Marie Félicité, attended the famous school at the Ursuline Convent in New Orleans, but not many of the children at the Post could have expected quite so advantageous a start in life.

No Post establishment was ever described as an inn or tavern, but there were any number of bars (*cabarets* and *cantinas*) and billiard halls, legal and illegal, where luxury goods like sugar and coffee, in addition to *tafia* (rum) and *eau de vie* (brandy), could be ordered up in a convivial surrounding; and probably a rudimentary meal and a bed could be found there or elsewhere for a sum, if a traveler did not have an introduction to a townsperson, or a boat that provided a reasonable refuge. The fort built in 1756 did have an outbuilding for temporarily housing crew members of the convoys that put in at the Post, and there was a similar structure for hosting Indian visitors. But these were very crude affairs and it is not clear that these kinds of accommodations were available during the late colonial era.

Ordinary folk consumed large amounts of cheap *tafia* and *eau de vie*, but those with more upscale tastes (and pocketbooks) drank wine—claret from the Médoc region of Bordeaux was an evident favorite. Sangaree, a fruit punch made with wine or rum, lent a somewhat tropical air to the frequent revelries at the Post. Arkansas residents exhibited considerable creativity when it came to devising drinks: A fine nog made from cranes' eggs is an example. Drinking was a common pastime, and medicinal purposes were sometimes wryly invoked as an excuse for it: A quantity of wine or liquor sufficient to induce a happy reverie or a dozing insensibility was dubbed "a mosquito dose," since it provided sweet respite from the intolerable stinging insects that infested the Arkansas region in swarms. One priest, venturing up to the Post from New Orleans in the 1720s, vouchsafed sardonically that Louisiana mosquitoes had caused more cursing than had occurred in the entire previous history of the world.

The diet of soldiers, hunters, and slaves featured venison, buffalo meat, and various corn dishes—among them cornbread of different kinds and a corn mush or porridge, called *sagamité* or *grú*, often seasoned with bear's oil and perhaps a little turkey or duck. The military gentry and the merchant class, in contrast, regularly tucked into meals that offered a much greater variety. Early in the morning, they had what they called a *café complet*, we call it a Continental breakfast, of wheat bread (cornbread being beneath them), butter, and coffee with cream and sugar. For the noon meal, called *diner*, the Post elite went all out and made full use of their orchards, kitchen gardens, and farm animals as well as game. Menus included wine and a number of meat dishes—hare, venison, ham, and beef, some stewed creole style with wine and herbs. A butter and cheese course with wheat bread and more wine followed. No evening meal has left a record, but it may often have been a *souper*, a light repast, as was the case elsewhere in the colony. These meals were prepared and served, and the courses cleared off, by household staff, usually Indian or African slaves.

The first African residents of Arkansas, perhaps no more than six altogether, had disembarked at the Post in 1721 when Law's workers revived the Arkansas settlement. The number of slaves at the Post was always small: The census of 1798 counted only 56 of them, black and mulatto, in a population of almost four hundred. Some had been born in Louisiana, and so were technically Creoles, but others may have been rather recently transported from Africa. They engaged in a wide range of activities. Many, like those who cooked and served up the varied fare at the houses of the grandees, were domestic servants; a large number, of course, worked in the fields. But some were skilled artisans. An old African blacksmith was resident at the Post in 1791, and others no doubt engaged in the building trades. A few, maybe one or two, of the Post's slaves were literate and may have worked as clerks in their masters' mercantile businesses, and still others acted as traders for their merchant masters. In 1779, for instance, two slaves named Louis and Sezar—the one born in New Orleans, the other in Guinea—had, on the orders of their master, Bentura Orueta, illegally sold liquor to some Abenaki Indians sojourning at the Post. The commandant opened criminal proceedings and, after he threatened the slaves with 100 lashes, they recanted a story that they and Orueta had concocted and they revealed Orueta's participation in their crime. The commandant jailed Orueta awaiting the orders of the governor. (It is interesting to see slaves' testimony used against their masters.)

When François Ménard died in 1791, some of his slaves requested four masses for the repose of their departed master's soul, and they paid Father Pierre Gibault, a missionary priest residing at the Post, the sum of two *pesos* in tobacco for celebrating them. The slaves' request perhaps indicates that they were at least superficially acculturated to Christian practices and also incidentally reveals that Arkansas slaves, in keeping with the custom throughout the colony, tilled their own plots of ground that produced profits they could spend as they wished. One way that slaves ardently wished to spend those profits was quite literally on themselves, because under Spanish law a slave had a right to purchase his own freedom; if the master refused to accept the price the slave offered, the slave could sue the master, have an appraiser appointed, and compel the master to accept the appraiser's price. We have no evidence of slaves at the Post taking advantage of this Spanish custom, but it would not be a cause for surprise if they did, since these self-purchases were common in the colony.

As we might expect, some Arkansas slaves were tempted to

Father Pierre Gibault, 1737–1802. Missouri History Museum, St. Louis

achieve their liberty without paying for it. Three or four of the widow Ménard's slaves, for instance, stole away to the Choctaws in 1792. Slave-catching was one of the commandants' duties, and they frequently paid the Quapaws for their help in arresting and returning runaways. (A Quapaw *métis* named Chalmet had wanted to keep a slave he captured, but the commandant ordered the slave's return.) Occasionally, a Quapaw or Post resident might catch a runaway whose master was unknown, in which case the commandant would do his best to locate the owner. In 1783, for example, Commandant Jacobo DuBreuil drafted what he styled a Notice of a Black Runaway Held in the Fort of Carlos III of Arkansas, which he presumably posted and sent to the governor for circulation to other towns and posts in Louisiana, and perhaps also to some of the territories and constituent republics of that new country called the United States. The notice contained the following description of the runaway:

> Cezar, a creole [*i.e.*, native] of Virginia, age twenty years more or less, with large eyes, well-shaped nostrils, long chin, and no beard, five feet and six inches tall, lean body, and suffering greatly from back pain. Arkansas, 1 August 1783.
>
> Jacobo Dubreuil

What the relatively rosy descriptions of the late colonial village omit, as do the official censuses for the most part, is the story of how a large portion, indeed a majority, of Arkansas's colonial denizens spent their lives. During the hunting season, roughly from October to April, normally beyond the census takers' watchful eyes, large numbers of hunting parties scoured the prairies, woods, and rivers for available game. In 1749, for instance, there were only 41 white people and 13 slaves residing at the settlement itself, but 65 *voyageur* hunters and *engagés* (hired hands) had remained stubbornly on the rivers despite the commandant's orders to return to the Post. In the late eighteenth century, upwards of two to three hundred hunting parties operated in the region, most outfitted at the Post, but some in Pointe Coupée, Ouachita Post, or even New Orleans. The hunters outnumbered the merchants and *habitants* throughout the colonial period, and many of the resident merchants and even a few *habitants* abandoned the Post in the fall to join in the annual hunt. One commandant in the 1790s said that his residents were "almost all hunters and always outdoors," and as late as 1802 an informed traveler claimed that for the six months of the hunting season one could find only women, children, and old men living in the village.

Some of these hunters ventured up the Arkansas River well into Oklahoma and Kansas—as far as 1000 miles upriver from the Post according to one report—and there they came into conflict with the mighty Osage nation, which did not take kindly to their poaching and dispatched them with some regularity. Probably as many as one hundred Arkansas hunters met their deaths this way during the eighteenth century, some in very gruesome circumstances. Even as late as the early nineteenth century, the Osages continued to kill and mutilate Frenchmen who trespassed on their game reserves.

Arkansas commandants and the governor in New Orleans made some fitful, mostly feckless attempts to curtail this slaughter, but they did not have the will—not to mention the troops or the ordnance—to overcome the powerful Osage tribe. A particularly pressing prudential matter was that the St. Louis merchants enjoyed mainly peaceful commercial relations with the Osages, and so they were more than cool to Spanish plans to cut off trade and wage war with the tribe. When one government official bloodlessly observed that the St. Louis trade was worth far more than the lives of a few Arkansas "scum," interlopers who were interfering with the official St. Louis oligopoly anyway, Post commandant Balthazar de Villiers memorably demanded whether commerce should be sealed with the blood of innocents. The New Orleans government offered no ready reply.

This is not to intimate that Arkansas commandants had any particular affection or respect for the hunters of the Arkansas in the abstract. Far from it. Because these hunters were their debtors, the commandants were forever in disputes with them, and the commandants' letters are full of complaints about the hunters' character:

Drawing by Alexandre De Batz showing Indians selling *plat côté* (buffalo ribs), *suif* (buffalo tallow), and *huille dourse* (bear's oil) in New Orleans, 1735. Peabody Museum, Harvard University.

They were deadbeats, professional drunks, frauds, swindlers, criminals, even scum. (No doubt the hunters cordially requited the commandants' disdain.) Villiers himself mocked them, saying that they owned nothing but their guns and did not know how to do anything but shoot them. Though Villiers's evaluation of the hunters was certainly harsh, he was right that they were generally destitute, as their estate inventories and visitors' descriptions of them reveal. Villiers lobbied the governor to close down the Post's bars and billiard halls because drink caused hunters to be forgetful debtors, and because they sometimes lost their money—money that might otherwise pay debts—in the gambling that was popular in those precincts.

It was not just the Osages who posed a threat to lives and livelihoods at the Arkansas. Other Indians harried the *habitants* of the

Post itself. One late colonial observer reported that Indians from east of the Mississippi, no doubt Choctaws and Chickasaws, driven from their usual haunts by the expanding American frontier, stole plow horses from the Post's farmers and sometimes filched the very crops themselves from the field. As a result, the observer said, the *habitants* near the village were all poor and miserable.

By the end of the colonial epoch, the larger merchants—there were four or five of them—would have carried some luxury goods like coffee and sugar along with staples like salt, rice, and flour; a small selection of fabrics, mosquito netting, and soap; building supplies including tools and nails; and perhaps a few manufactured goods like shoes and boots. But their main stock-in-trade was hunting supplies, for the Post's principal economic activity was tied to products of the hunt—some deerskins and other pelts, but, for most of the eighteenth century, mainly salted buffalo meat (ribs and tongues), buffalo tallow, and bear's oil. So the merchants of the colonial Post dealt chiefly in guns, powder, balls, blankets, cauldrons, and even in horses, mules, and saddles. They advanced most of these goods on credit to hunters who, ideally, would pay their debts in the product from their expeditions before taking what was left over, if anything, to New Orleans (the *ville*) to sell. There they could have a high old time in the numerous dives in the back of the city. Or they could go all out at one of the more posh watering places, like the one on Royal Street kept by a man named Barté, who advertised in the *Moniteur de La Louisane* that he was a *traiteur et pâtissier* (caterer and confectioner) and kept an inn with a *table d'Hôte* (public dining room). Barté even prepared *des repas pour le dehors*—presumably meals for events off premises.

The merchants were therefore merchant-capitalists and it is a nice question whether they were in the business of selling supplies, or products of the hunt, or credit. The truth is that they sold all three. To make matters a little more complex, some of them were also *habitants* who sold their agricultural surplus either locally or downriver. As we saw, the widow Ménard, with nine black slaves, was the largest slaveholder at the Post in 1791 but was listed as a merchant and produced no crop that year; two years later, however, she was one of the four or five most productive farmers in the village, growing all three cash crops—wheat, corn, and tobacco. It seems plain that she had not switched occupations but over the years had been engaged in both trade and agriculture—in short, she was simultaneously a merchant, planter, and proto-banker.

What to the modern mind may be the oddest thing about the economic and governmental arrangements at the Post was that the commandant there was very active as a merchant. True, he was always a military officer—a French marine or a Spanish army officer depending on who was claiming sovereignty—and he was the head of the local government, serving as commander-in-chief of the armed forces and ambassador to foreign nations (particularly Indian ones). He was the civil and military judge, he acted as the Post's notary (a non-forensic lawyer and recorder of documents), and he gathered evidence for and executed the judgments of the courts in New Orleans. The commandant, in short, was the government personified and of course he received a governmental emolument for his services.

But the commandant was also a person of considerable social rank and quality, sometimes even from a noble family (though no one at the Arkansas was titled), and he was used to a certain standard of living; so the government allowed him to engage in business to supplement the meager crust that it allowed him in salary. He engaged in a mercantile business in competition with the Post's residents, and, at least during the Spanish period, he acted as the garrison's sutler, supplying the soldiers' rations and receiving compensation at a fixed rate per soldier. Sometimes, the government even allowed him a monopoly on the trade with certain Indian tribes. Many commandants thus prospered, though some few wound up bankrupt. Advancing goods to hunters and Indians was a risky business, and markets were unreliable anyway. But there were times when the Arkansas Post was among the most attractive duty stations in the colony because of trade opportunities there. Even noncommissioned officers could profit handsomely from a stint at the Post. In the 1770s, Sergeant Francis Vigo, an Italian who served in the Spanish garrison at the Arkansas, became associated with Fernando de Leyba, the Post commandant, and traded upriver for him. Vigo followed Leyba to the Illinois country, became a very wealthy fur trader in St. Louis and Vincennes, and wound up a major financier of the American revolutionary effort. In 1986, the United States Government issued a commemorative postcard in his honor bearing his likeness, and there is a large statue of him in Vincennes.

Ste. Genevieve was a farming community, and so local police regulations there focused mainly on agricultural pursuits, especially on governing the operation of the *grand champ*—the compound of arable fields that the *habitants* shared. But there was no common field at the Post, and Arkansas commandants' ordinances tended rather to deal with regulating hunting and trading there—as we would expect, since those were the activities that sustained the Post's economy. For instance, in 1783 Captain Jacobo Dubreuil

Francis Vigo, 1747–1836, ca. 1820. Vincennes University.

published an order, evidently in response to a disaster that had resulted from Christmas revelling, that read:

> Don Jacobo Dubreuil, Captain of Infantry and Commandant of the Post and District of Arkansas: In order to avoid the accidents that occur frequently on account of unexpected fires at this place, and on account of the dangers that drunken Indians or evil-intentioned persons who commit criminal acts create, I order that there cannot be more than six pounds of powder in any house of this place. And to effect this order, persons who have a quantity of powder that exceeds the aforesaid six pounds shall take it all to the king's warehouse today, and the owner of it shall put a tag with his name [on his barrel] along with the weight of the barrel and its contents, and second corporal Lucas Perez will receive it after verifying the said weight. It is to be understood that every time that the said owner wants to dispense his powder to hunters he can present himself [to the warehouse] at convenient times. In order to have this order observed

> by travelers as well as those who reside at this post, travelers must take their munitions to the aforesaid warehouse immediately upon arrival.
>
> Arkansas, 26 December 1783
> Jacobo Dubreuil

In 1778 and 1798, moreover, what the French of the Post referred to as ordinances were promulgated that established priorities between merchants who supplied hunters and the hunters' *engagés*, and created appropriate liens to enforce these obligations. An interesting feature of the 1798 ordinance is that it was worked out by the commandant in consultation with two persons each from the hunter and merchant classes. It included some fines for its violation. These kinds of business regulations are not merely intrinsically interesting, though they are certainly that. They are also revealing for the light they shed on the suppositions that gave shape to colonial Louisiana government and society. There was never a specific grant of legislative authority to Post commandants as far as we know, but such was the hierarchal character of colonial Louisiana society that it was simply assumed that the patriarchal commandant had the power, indeed the duty, to create an efficient and moral social arrangement for his inhabitants. So, in many cases, commandants simply issued decrees and expected obedience. But the quasi-democractic process that led to the 1798 ordinance, particularly the commandant's consultation with representatives of affected constituents, intimates that the customary powers of village assemblies in France had found a place in the governmental structure at the Post, or perhaps even that eighteenth-century republicanism had gained some purchase in colonial Arkansas.

The social background of the Louisiana military officers accounts for the fact, at first almost unbelievable, that upwards of a dozen eighteenth-century portraits of Arkansas commandants, their wives, and their family members, all of whom lived at the Post, have come down to us. Perhaps an equal number have perished or disappeared into secret family recesses in Louisiana, France, or Spain. Some of these portraits were paid for partly by the proceeds from trading on the Arkansas River. Chief among the products exchanged was salted buffalo meat. Buffalo could be found all over the state, along the river valleys, around the salines, and on the prairies: *Vache grasse* (fat cow) prairie in northwest Arkansas must have taken its name from the abundance of female buffalo to be had there; the ribs from the buffalo cow's hump were the most sought-after cut of the beast because of their toothsome succulence.

Buffalo tongues, too, were a great delicacy. In the late eighteenth century, a traveler reported that two hundred buffalo carcasses had been left behind to rot in the St. Francis River region after the tongues had been cut out. Salted buffalo tongues, coupled with pecans from the same St. Francis River valley, made a big hit in New Orleans, and even in Madrid, when Arkansas commandants remembered to send them to their superiors as a compliment. (A New York delicatessen might find these items readily saleable today.) Less exotic parts of the animal were salted and shipped downriver to feed slaves, soldiers, and other less affluent colonials. Buffalo tallow was also in demand. Though it had a variety of uses, it was frequently mixed with myrtle wax and made into candles. It was also used to caulk boats: The Post merchant François Ménard once landed a contract for 10,000 pounds of the stuff for use in the Havana shipyards.

But bear's oil was probably the most versatile of Arkansas's exports. It was used as salad dressing and as a cooking oil—much preferable to lard, the colonists said. In the winter, when it hardened, it was spread on bread like butter. It was also used for seasoning corn and meat dishes, for softening skins, as a hair oil, as a base for face paint, as a balm for rheumatism, even as a mosquito repellent applied to the skin. But it probably found its most general use fueling the lamps of the colony. Large amounts of it were sold to the colonial government in the 1790s for use in its buildings and in the new streetlights that illuminated what is now the French Quarter in New Orleans.

Some of the hunters and merchants of the Arkansas were engaged in a much more nefarious trade: trafficking in human beings, mostly Indian women and children. These traffickers provided guns, ammunition, and manufactured goods to the Osage tribe in return for horses, mules, and Indian captives whom the Osages took from the Wichita and Caddo villages. The hunters used the horses to hunt buffalo, the mules as pack animals, and their human haul as concubines and workers. Sometimes, white and *mestiza* women stolen by Comanches from New Mexico and sold to the Wichitas would be resold to Arkansas hunters. Many of these women were subject to horrendous abuse by their Indian captors and probably by some of their French ones as well.

In the very late colonial period, say, around the end of the eighteenth century, due mainly to a vigorous if sporadic trade with the powerful Osage nation, a band of which lived high up the Arkansas River, the pelt and skin trade probably came to dominate Arkansas exports. Deer, bear, beaver, otter, fox, wild cat, racoon, and other furs were shipped to New Orleans on the boats of Post merchants.

That these objects of colonial Arkansas commerce fueled the production of eighteenth-century portraiture at first seems improbable. But it is demonstrably true, and no more improbable really than the exotic nature of the commerce itself—or, for that matter, than the fact that people with such backgrounds as those whom the portraits portray ventured into the swamps and forests of eighteenth-century Arkansas at all. Perhaps the aristocratic colonial women will seem to us the most unlikely denizens of such a place, especially when we see them posing serenely in their finery. Though some officers' wives stayed in New Orleans during their husband's sojourn at the Post, an assignment that usually lasted only a few years, most of them accompanied their husbands to the Arkansas country, and some even gave birth in the commandant's house at the Post.

One such birth occurred on 23 September 1732, when Marie Françoise Petit de Coulange, the daughter of First Ensign Pierre Louis Petit de Coulange, drew her first breath shortly after her father assumed his duties as Post commandant. Her tombstone in a New Orleans cemetery records this event in French, noting that she was *née aux Arkansas* (born at the Arkansas). The Post was often called *Poste aux Arks*, an abbreviation of *Poste aux Arkansas*, and this is the origin of the word Ozark. (We have been speaking French all these years and did not know it.) The Chickasaws killed Marie's father in 1739 during Governor Bienville's unsuccessful war against them. Some said he was burned at the stake.

Marie moved to New Orleans with her mother, was orphaned at a very young age, and eventually married three times before becoming a confirmed widow in her thirty-ninth year. She celebrated her last nuptials just outside Versailles, and it is probable that her portrait was painted in or somewhere near that city in the early

Marie Françoise de Coulange de Vilemont, 1732–1812, ca. 1765.
The Historic New Orleans Collection.

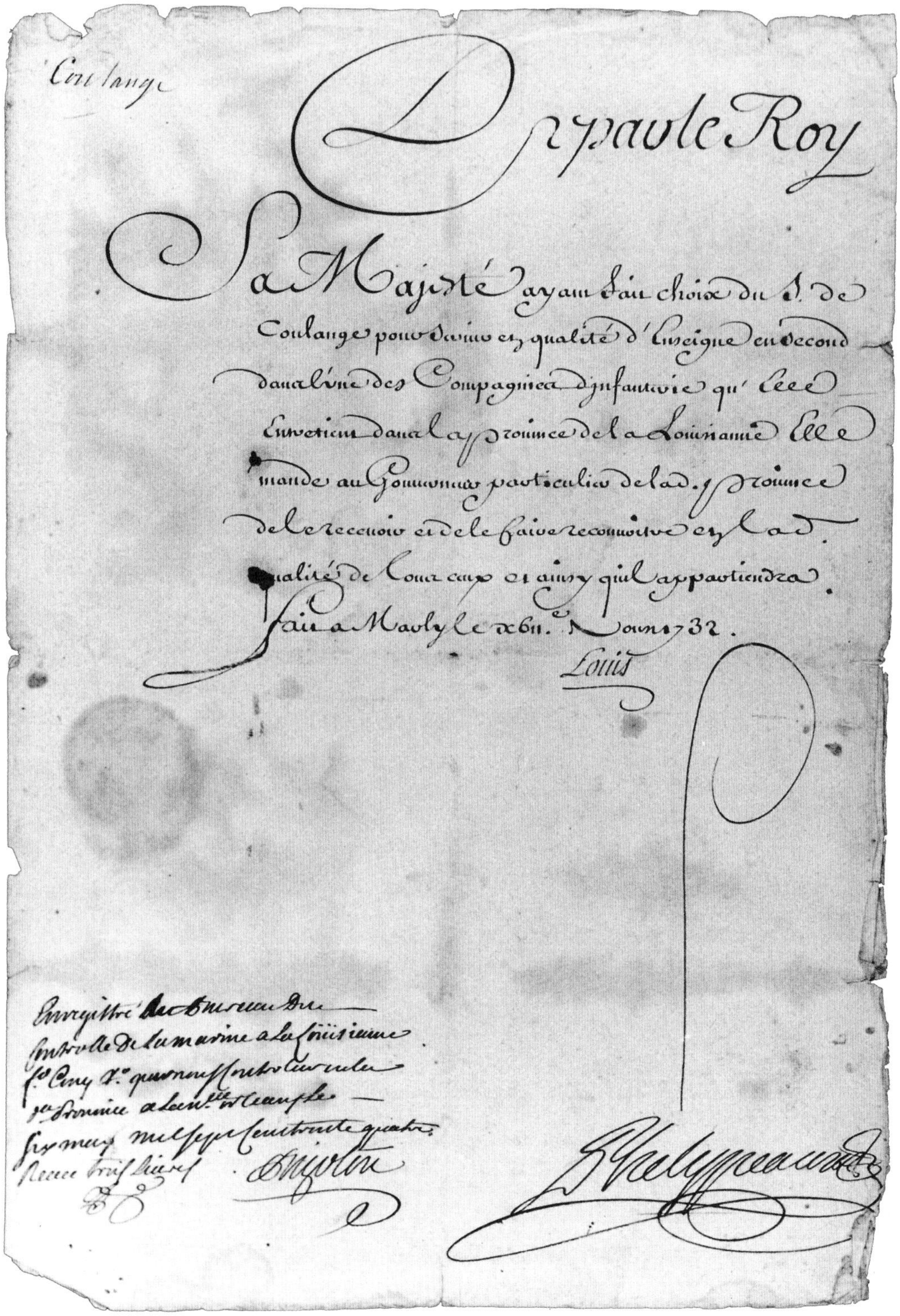

Coulange

De par le Roy

Sa Majesté ayant fait choix du S. de Coulange pour servir en qualité d'Enseigne en second dans l'une des Compagnies d'infanterie qu'elle entretient dans la province de la Louisiane Elle mande au Gouverneur particulier de lad. province de le recevoir et de le faire reconnoitre en lad. qualité de tous ceux et ainsy qu'il appartiendra. Fait a Marly le xvii.e Nov. 1732.

Louis

Phelypeaux

Pierre Petit de Coulange's commission from Louis XV, 1732.
The Historic New Orleans Collection.

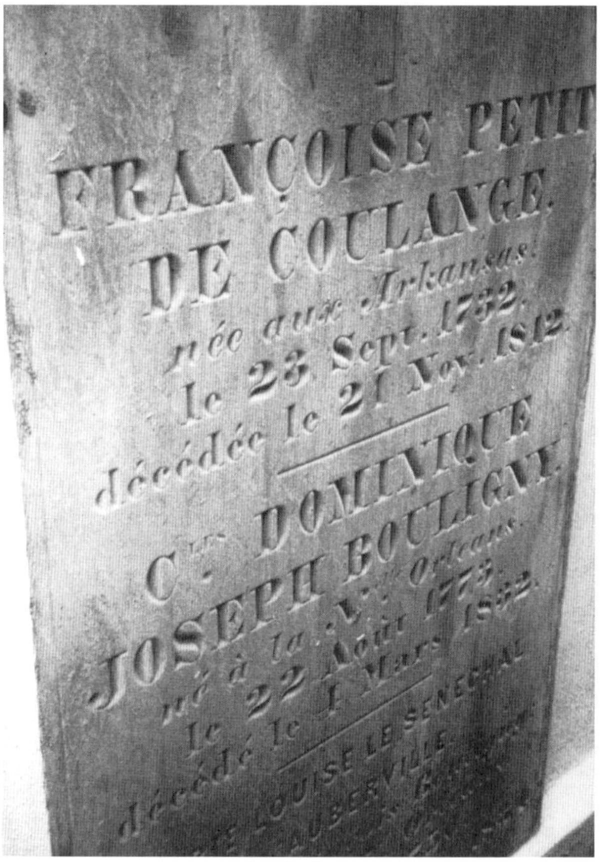

Marie Françoise Petit de Coulange's tombstone, New Orleans. Photo by Gail K. Arnold.

1760s. Marie's son, Charles Melchior de Vilemont, was commandant of the Post from 1794 to 1802. His portrait shows him at about thirteen years of age in the uniform of a cadet in the Fixed Regiment of Louisiana and was probably painted in France or in Spain when he was attending a Spanish military academy for members of noble families. A town in Chicot County once bore his name.

Three other portraits are of a piece. Captain Alexandre Chevalier DeClouet, one of the first Post commandants of the Spanish era, wrote highly literate letters from the Post's downriver location, and was sufficiently well connected to arrange to have his wife's brother, Pierre-Joseph Favrot, an army officer, transferred to his remote command. DeClouet's wife, Louise Farrot, distinguished herself by ministering to the sick who had been brought

Louise Favrot, 1737–1814, ca. 1780. Private collection of Favrot family.

into the fort during an epidemic, and she left some unspecified ornaments for the Post's chapel when she and her husband left in 1769. "Ornament" is an ecclesiastical term of art that is broad enough to include crosses, candlesticks, vessels, cruets, statues, altar cloths, or even vestments. Louise DeClouet had the means,

Pierre-Joseph Favrot, 1749–1824, ca. 1795. Attributed to José Salazar. Private collection of Favrot family.

and the taste, to have provided any of a range of significant gifts to the little chapel, for we know that she bought prodigious quantities of silver, fancy dresses, and fine linens at her mother's estate sale in New Orleans. Some of these luxury items may well have found their way up the river to Louise's temporary Arkansas abode. Her

Marie Madeleine Broutin Delinó de Chalmette, died 1805, ca. 1760.
The Historic New Orleans Collection.

brother, Pierre-Joseph, was a gentleman of culture and refinement, proof of which comes from a little manual that he wrote for the education of his sons outlining what an educated Creole gentleman should know. He pointedly noted that a knowledge of Latin was absolutely essential.

Victoire Delinó de Chalmette, 1777–1868, ca. 1795.
Private collection of Reinecke family.

Another very early colonial resident of Arkansas Post was Marie Madeleine Broutin Delinó de Chalmette, the wife of the Post commandant when the Chickasaws attacked the fort in 1749, killed a few male *habitants*, and carried off a number of women and children, most of whom were later ransomed. Marie's portrait was probably painted in Paris around 1760. (One of her granddaughters became the Baroness de Pontalba, who is famous, among other things, for erecting the exquisite apartment buildings that flank Jackson Square in New Orleans.) Marie provides another example of the interconnections among Arkansas's ruling class, for her son, Jean Ignace Delinó de Chalmette, served as Post commandant from 1790 to 1794. The battle of New Orleans would be fought at his plantation in Chalmette, Louisiana, about twenty years after he left the Arkansas. His daughter, Victoire Delinó de Chalmette, spent a few years as a child at the Post. When she returned to

Tombstone of Amelia Gocio (Gossiau), St. Peter's Cemetery, New Gascony, Arkansas. Photo by Gail K. Arnold.

Tombstone of Mary Ann Valliere, St. Peter's cemetery, New Gascony, Arkansas. Photo by Gail K. Arnold.

New Orleans after her father's tour of duty at the Post expired, her mother heaved a great sigh of relief because little Victoire could now enjoy the cultural advantages of the *ville*, including music lessons and dancing lessons.

The nineteenth century dawned on an isolated Arkansas Post of Louisiana that was surprisingly cosmopolitan. A traveler walking through the creole village might, in short order and in a very small space, have heard people conversing in French, Spanish, English, and German. A number of Indian languages might also have reached the traveler's ear, chiefly Quapaw, but others as well, probably including Mobilian, the Indian trade language. Indian slaves and Indian wives of French hunters spoke their native tongues. One Post denizen claimed to be fluent in four Indian languages, probably including Caddo and Chickasaw. One of Bentura Orueta's black slaves, it was said, even spoke Abenaki. The black slaves conversed in an Afro-creole *patois*, their version of French, and some no doubt retained a knowledge of an African language or two. The polyglot population at the eighteenth-century Arkansas Post of Louisiana produced a veritable tower of Babel, which at this distance can only cause us finally to wonder and admire.

Iron crosses in Natchitoches colonial Cemetery.
Photo by Gail K. Arnold.

POSTSCRIPT

THE POST'S POPULATION could not have much exceeded 400 souls, and there were not many more than 500 Quapaws in the neighborhood, when an American army lieutenant with a sergeant, two corporals, and 11 soldiers took over the fort there on 23 March 1804. Such was the indifference of the Spanish king to the whole enterprise that only three Spanish soldiers and their captain had stayed behind to see that the exchange went properly. But the coming of the Americans brought a great deal more to the French inhabitants of Arkansas than a formal substitution of sovereigns. The ancient residents very soon found themselves in a decided minority and the newcomers were not all well disposed to them. Some of the newly arrived ridiculed the French for their "superstitious" religion and their patriarchal political and legal system. They sneered at their lack of medical science, though American medicine was by no means more advanced. Americans repeatedly criticized what they considered French "indolence" and were censorious of their gambling and dancing; they even spoke deprecatingly of the style and construction of Louisiana houses. Segregated on account of their language, customs, and manners, the French were virtually excluded from participation in government: They only very rarely served on juries and almost never sought political office. The Quapaws suffered a worse kind of discrimination, a kind known to all manner of Indian people. Their new government banished them entirely to Indian territory, and not a few of them found death awaiting them along the way.

In 1819, when the Post became the capital of the newly minted Arkansas Territory, there were still only fifty or sixty families living there or in its vicinity and twenty-five or thirty houses in the village proper. The *Arkansas Gazette* began publishing at the Post in the same year, but the removal of the territorial capital (and the newspaper) to Little Rock in 1821 did nothing to lift the settlement's prospects. It remained a small town of a few hundred people with a steamboat landing and a bank, soon reduced to a backwater by the flood of American immigration. Washington Irving and other literary visitors in the 1830s and 1840s rhapsodized romantically over the dilapidated colonial houses at the Post, some fully six feet off the ground with galleries all around, just like the ones Captain Rousseau had seen in 1793, relics of a lost French empire, that gave the Post a haunting, antiquated air. Some of these ruinous souvenirs of colonial days survived until 1863, when Union gunboats pummeled them all to rubble in yet another Battle of Arkansas Post, this one the third and by far the most deadly. Still, the Post struggled on as a tiny village of perhaps one hundred people and two or three stores well into the twentieth century. In 1934, the United States Post Office, which had opened there in 1817, closed its doors; it reopened a year or two later, hoping against hope, only to flicker out again, this time for good, in 1941.

In 1960, though, the United States came back and replaced an underfunded state park that, in an admirable effort to commemorate the settlement's history, had been established at the Post thirty years before. Today, the Arkansas Post National Memorial stands guard over the old town site. It features a fine brick building, ironically a good deal more elaborate than any structure the actual Post had ever seen, that flies six flags, one for each sovereign that had claimed to hold sway over the region. Inside, interpretive exhibits and a movie tell the story of the Post. Outside, visitors, helped along by explanatory panels that guide the imagination, can stroll the ground where the settlement once sat. But the Arkansas Post of Louisiana itself, though it had breathed the air of four different centuries, has disappeared completely, the victim of war, the relentless river, and the malice of time.

Iron cross, St. Mary's churchyard,
Plum Bayou, Arkansas.
Photo by Gail K. Arnold.